# A Midsummer Night's Dream

An imprint of Om Books International

It was time for celebrations. The Duke of Athens, Theseus was to marry the Queen of the Amazons, Hippolyta. A four-day festival was planned.

A nobleman called Egeus visited Theseus's court with his daughter, Hermia and two young men called Lysander and Demetrius. Egeus wanted his daughter to marry Demetrius, who loved her.

But Hermia loved Lysander and refused to obey her father. Egeus wanted the Duke's help.

"If you disobey your father, you could be sent to a convent or even killed," Theseus warned Hermia and gave her time to decide till the date of his wedding.

Upset, Hermia and Lysander decided to elope from Athens that night and confided in Hermia's friend, Helena.

Helena had once been engaged to Demetrius, but he had broken off the engagement after he fell in love with Hermia. Helena still loved Demetrius and told him about Hermia and Lysander's plans.

Demetrius followed the couple as they escaped into the woods. Helena followed Demetrius in turn.

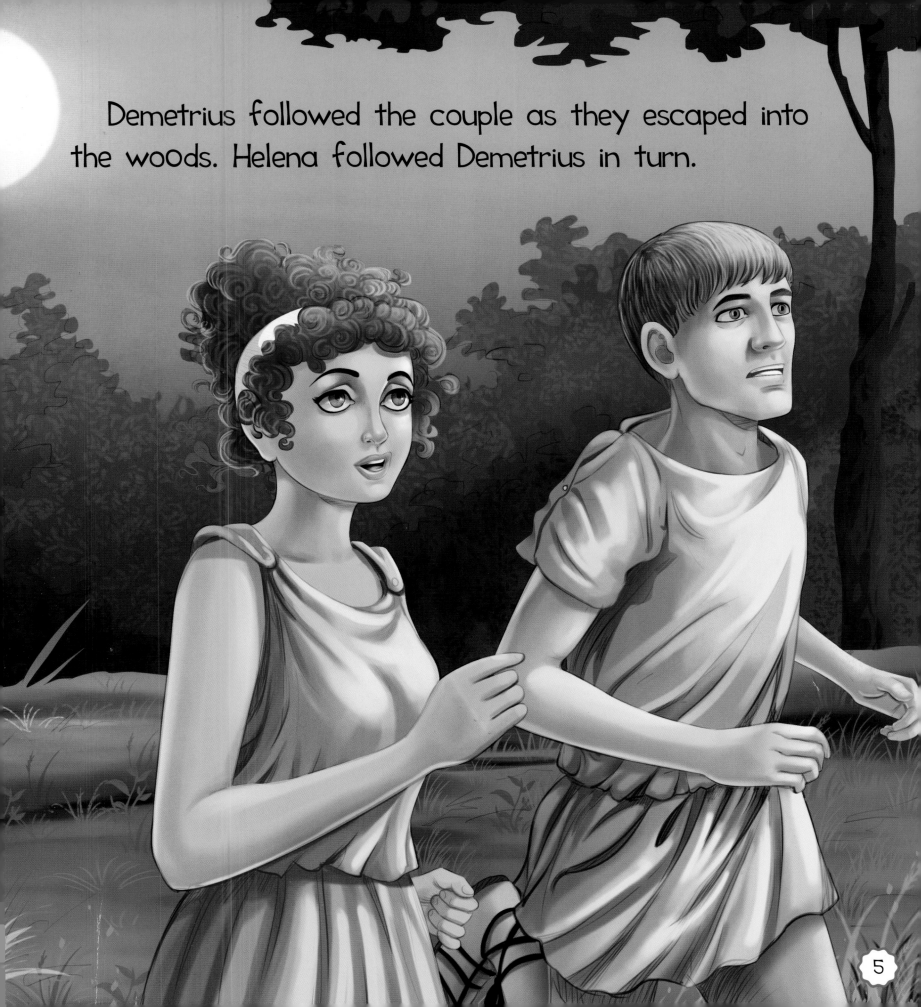

Besides these young people, two groups were present in the woods and each group was different from the other. One was an Athenian theatre group comprising craftsmen rehearsing a play that they intended to perform at the Duke's wedding.

The second was a band of fairies, including their King Oberon and Queen Titania. Oberon and Titania had quarrelled over a young prince who had been a gift to Titania.

Oberon wanted the prince to join his knights and Titania had refused.

As revenge, Oberon ordered his mischievous servant Puck to fetch a magical flower. "The potion from this flower, when applied over a sleeping person's eyelids, will make that person fall in love with the first thing he or she sees on waking up," Oberon explained to Puck.

"Apply this on Titania's eyelids when she is asleep," he ordered. Oberon had earlier seen Demetrius behave badly with Helena. So, Oberon asked Puck to apply the potion on the eyelids of the young Athenian man in the woods.

After putting the love potion on Titania's eyelids, Puck saw Lysander sleeping and mistook him for Demetrius and applied the potion! When he woke up, Lysander spotted Helena and fell madly in love with her.

Puck realised his mistake and put the potion on Demetrius's eyelids. Demetrius too saw Helena on waking up. Both Demetrius and Lysander professed their love for her. A jealous Hermia challenged Helena to a fight.

Puck tried to rectify his mistakes as the night progressed. He tricked Demetrius and Lysander away from each other as they prepared to fight a duel for Helena. He mimicked their voices till the two men were lost in the woods.

Meanwhile, Titania awoke to spot Bottom, the stupidest of the theatre actors, practising their play in the forest. Under Oberon's orders, the naughty Puck had transformed Bottom's head to that of a donkey and placed him before the sleeping Titania.

13

Titania fell in love with the donkey-headed weaver when she awoke and looked rather silly doting on him. Oberon decided that it was enough punishment for Titania and ordered Puck to reverse the spells on Titania and Lysander.

By morning, everything was normal again. Only Demetrius was still in love with Helena. They were found in the forest by Theseus and Hippolyta, who took them back to Athens to be married.

Lysander was now in love with Hermia and Demetrius loved Helena. After their wedding, the newly married couples sat together and watched the play performed by Bottom and his fellow artistes.

"It all appears to be a dream," Puck said to Oberon, "a midsummer night's dream!"

# Julius Caesar

An imprint of Om Books International

Many Roman citizens had gathered on the streets to watch Julius Caesar's victory parade. Caesar had won the battle against the sons of the dead Roman General Pompey. But, many in Rome were upset at their deaths.

Caesar and his associates, Brutus, Antony, Cassius and others, arrived with great pomp.

"Beware the Ides of March," a soothsayer shouted, warning Caesar about the fifteenth of March. But, Caesar ignored him and moved on.

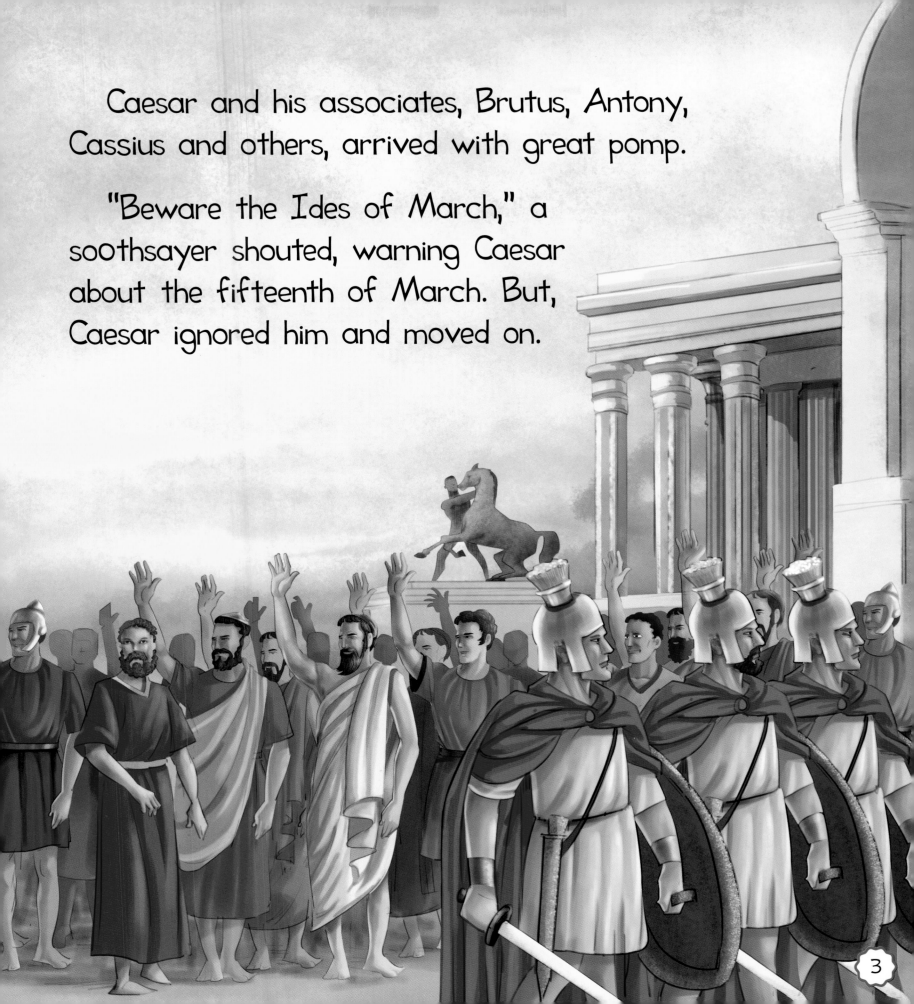

Cassius led the conspirators who wanted to kill Caesar. He asked Brutus to join them.

"Caesar is treated like a God, but he's just a man," Cassius said.

"People want Caesar to become king," Brutus replied. Cassius said all of them were to be blamed for Caesar's rise to power.

Meanwhile, Caesar confided to Antony that he did not trust Cassius. Another conspirator called Casca informed Brutus and Cassius that Antony had offered the crown to Caesar thrice during the celebrations. But, Caesar had refused it.

That night, bad weather and many bad omens spelled doom for Rome's future. Brutus found letters by citizens worrying about Caesar becoming too powerful. But these letters by citizens had been planted by Cassius.

6

Fear of Caesar's tyranny, pushed Brutus to join the conspirators. And soon, Cassius and other conspirators arrived at Brutus's house to plan Caesar's assassination. Cassius wanted to kill Antony too, but Brutus was against it. The conspirators left and Brutus was lost in thought.

Next morning, Caesar's wife, Calpurnia, urged him not to leave for the Senate. "I've had nightmares. Your statue was bathed in blood with smiling men washing their hands on it," she said. Caesar refused her request and one of the conspirators, Decius, convinced Caesar that she had misinterpreted the dream.

A few of the conspirators escorted Caesar to the Senate. The soothsayer tried to reach him but failed. A well-wisher handed Caesar a warning letter, but Caesar refused to read it and said, "My personal concerns are my last priority."

The conspirators surrounded Caesar at the Senate and stabbed him, one by one. Caesar stopped struggling when he saw his friend Brutus among them. "You too, Brutus?" Caesar exclaimed right before he died.

Antony, who had been led away, returned to sob at Caesar's death but pretended loyalty to Brutus. He requested to speak at Caesar's funeral where Brutus would explain why they had killed Caesar. Cassius was suspicious, but Brutus assured him that he would speak first.

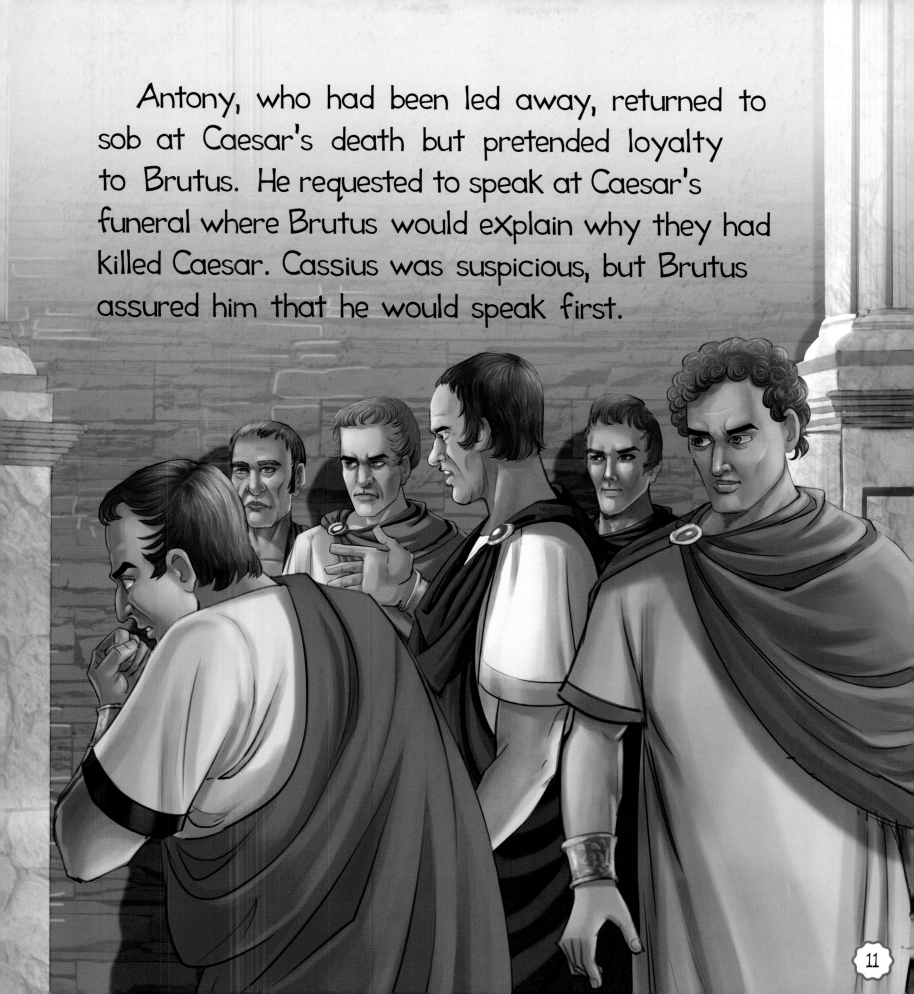

"I loved Caesar, but I love Rome more," Brutus addressed the crowd at the funeral. "Caesar was killed his ambition was dangerous to Roman freedom."

The crowd seemed satisfied with Brutus's speech.

Then, Antony came with Caesar's body. Addressing Brutus continuously as 'an honourable man', he spoke with sarcasm. Antony blasted the conspirators. "If Caesar was ambitious, why did he refuse the throne thrice? Hadn't Caesar brought glory to Rome?"

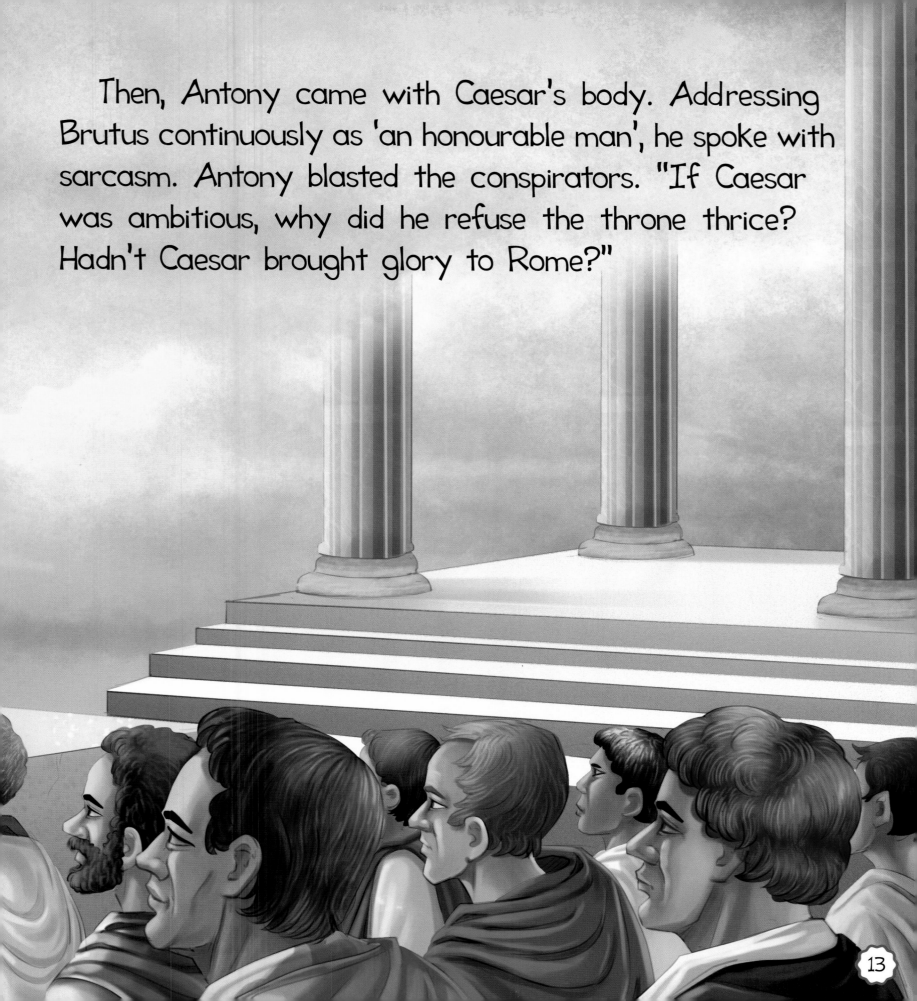

Antony displayed Caesar's body to the crowd and read aloud Caesar's will. Caesar had left his wealth to the people of Rome. The crowd was now furious with the conspirators and attacked them. But, they managed to escape.

Caesar's adopted son Octavius, along with Antony and Lepidus, raised an army to fight the conspirators. In the battlefield, Cassius and Brutus took their own lives when their armies were defeated.

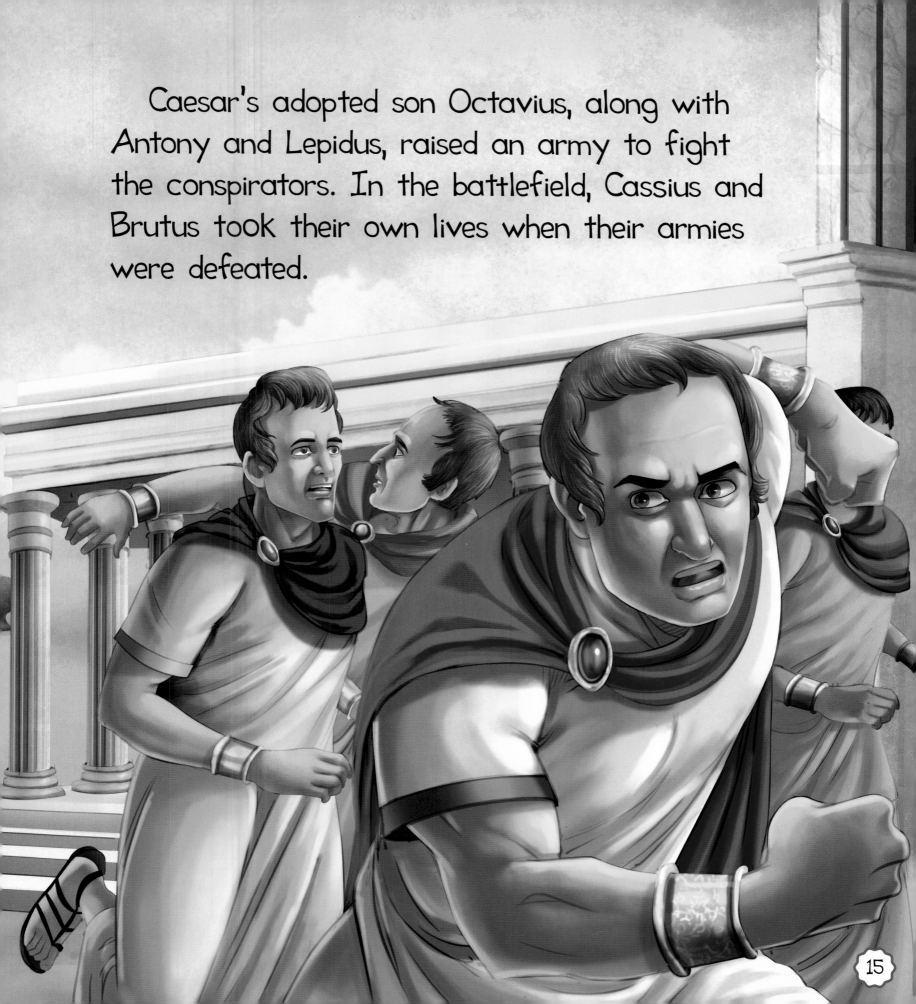

"While the other conspirators had acted selfishly, Brutus alone acted in Rome's interests," Antony said over Brutus's dead body. "Here lies the noblest Roman of them all."

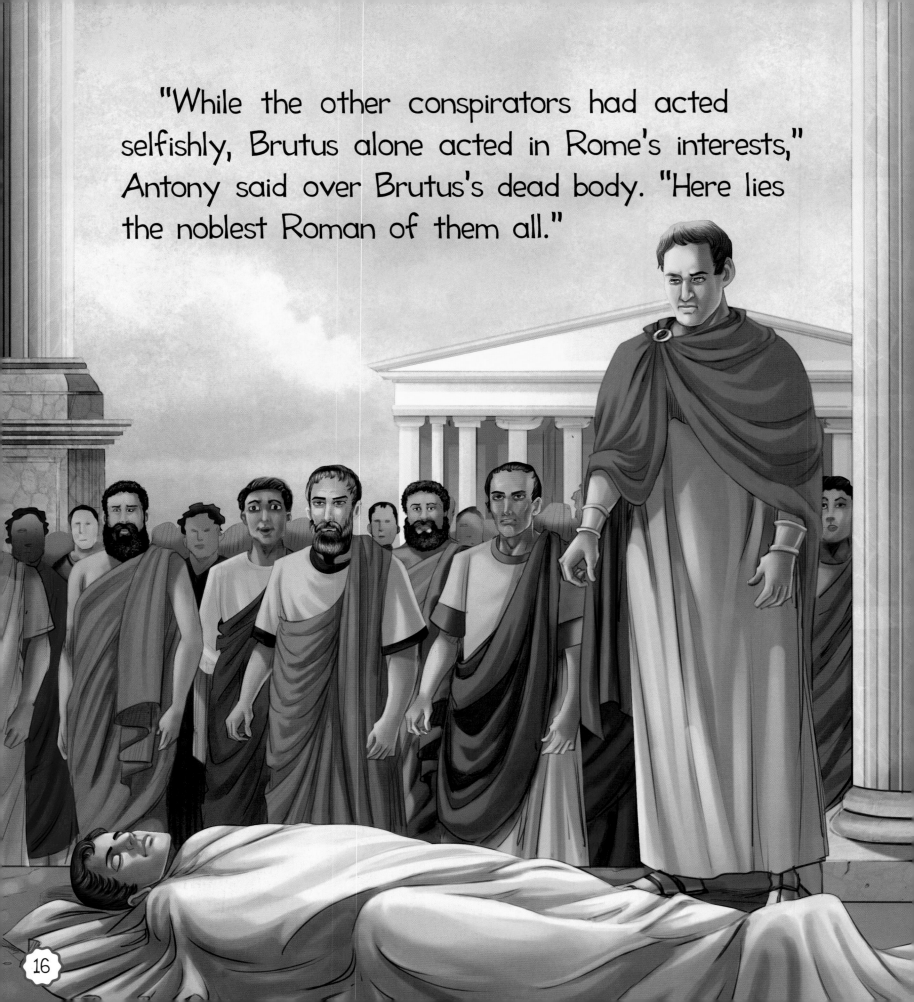

# Macbeth

An imprint of Om Books International

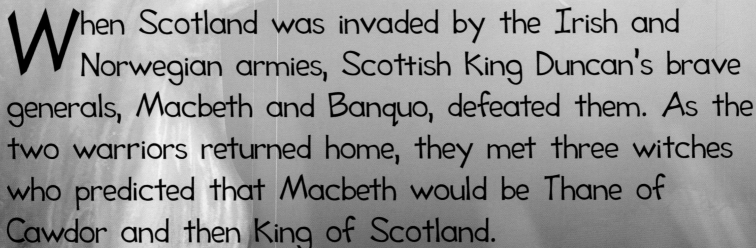

When Scotland was invaded by the Irish and Norwegian armies, Scottish King Duncan's brave generals, Macbeth and Banquo, defeated them. As the two warriors returned home, they met three witches who predicted that Macbeth would be Thane of Cawdor and then King of Scotland.

But they also predicted that Banquo would never be king and his heirs would rule over Scotland. Saying this, the witches vanished. Macbeth and Banquo didn't take their prophecies seriously and travelled on.

They were greeted with great pomp and King Duncan's men informed Macbeth that he had been made Thane of Cawdor for his bravery. King Duncan also sent a message that he would visit Inverness, Macbeth's castle, that night.

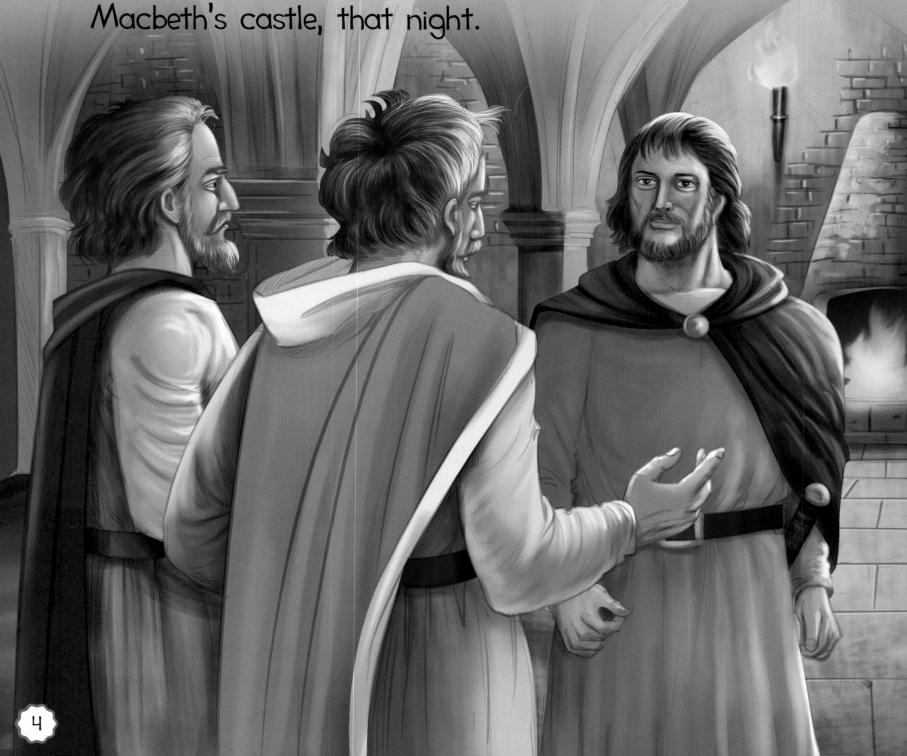

"Will I be crowned king?" Macbeth wondered.

At Inverness, the ambitious Lady Macbeth learnt about the prophecies and was determined that her husband should become the king.

"The King has to be murdered!" she insisted and convinced Macbeth to kill Duncan in his sleep.

"We shall get the chamberlains drunk and blame them for the murder," she plotted. Macbeth was haunted by doubts and supernatural visions, but managed to do the deed.

He stabbed Duncan in his sleep after the King's chamberlains had passed out. After Duncan's body was discovered, as planned, Macbeth killed the chamberlains. Fearing for their lives, Duncan's sons, Malcolm and Donalbain, ran away to England, and Macbeth ascended the throne.

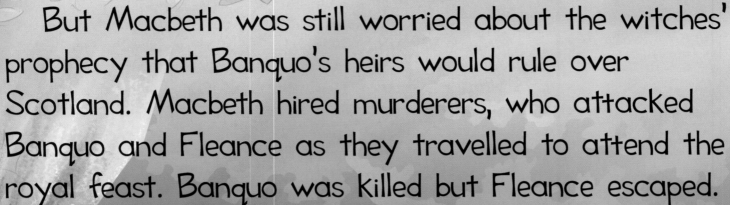

But Macbeth was still worried about the witches' prophecy that Banquo's heirs would rule over Scotland. Macbeth hired murderers, who attacked Banquo and Fleance as they travelled to attend the royal feast. Banquo was killed but Fleance escaped.

Banquo's ghost visited the feast that night, but only Macbeth could see him. A scared Macbeth ranted on and on to the gathering, shocking his guests who now suspected Macbeth's hand in the murders. Lady Macbeth tried to reassure the guests, but was unsuccessfull.

On facing opposition from the Scottish nobility and his subjects, Macbeth visited the witches and received further prophecies.

"Beware of Macduff!" the first witch said. Macduff was a nobleman who had opposed Macbeth as king.

"You cannot be killed by any man, who is born of a woman," the second witch predicted.

"You shall not be harmed until Birnam Wood come to Dunsinane Castle," the third witch said.

"I am safe," Macbeth thought. "Nonetheless, I must kill Macduff!"

Macbeth was furious when he learnt that Macduff had escaped to England to join Malcolm.

"Seize his castle and kill his wife and children," Macbeth ordered. A devastated Macduff swore revenge on Macbeth.

Meanwhile, Malcolm had raised an army in England and Macduff joined him as they marched towards Scotland to fight Macbeth's army. The Scottish nobles, who were tired of Macbeth's tyrannical rule, supported them. But as Macbeth became stronger, Lady Macbeth became weak and started to hallucinate. She saw bloodstains on her hands, where there was none, and began to sleepwalk.

Lady Macbeth finally committed suicide and Macbeth went into mourning. But soon he recovered and got ready to meet Malcolm's army. He thought that the witches' prophecies had made him invincible. But he was shocked when he heard that Birnam Wood was moving towards Dunsinane. Actually, the English soldiers had shielded themselves with branches and leaves taken from the woods as they advanced.

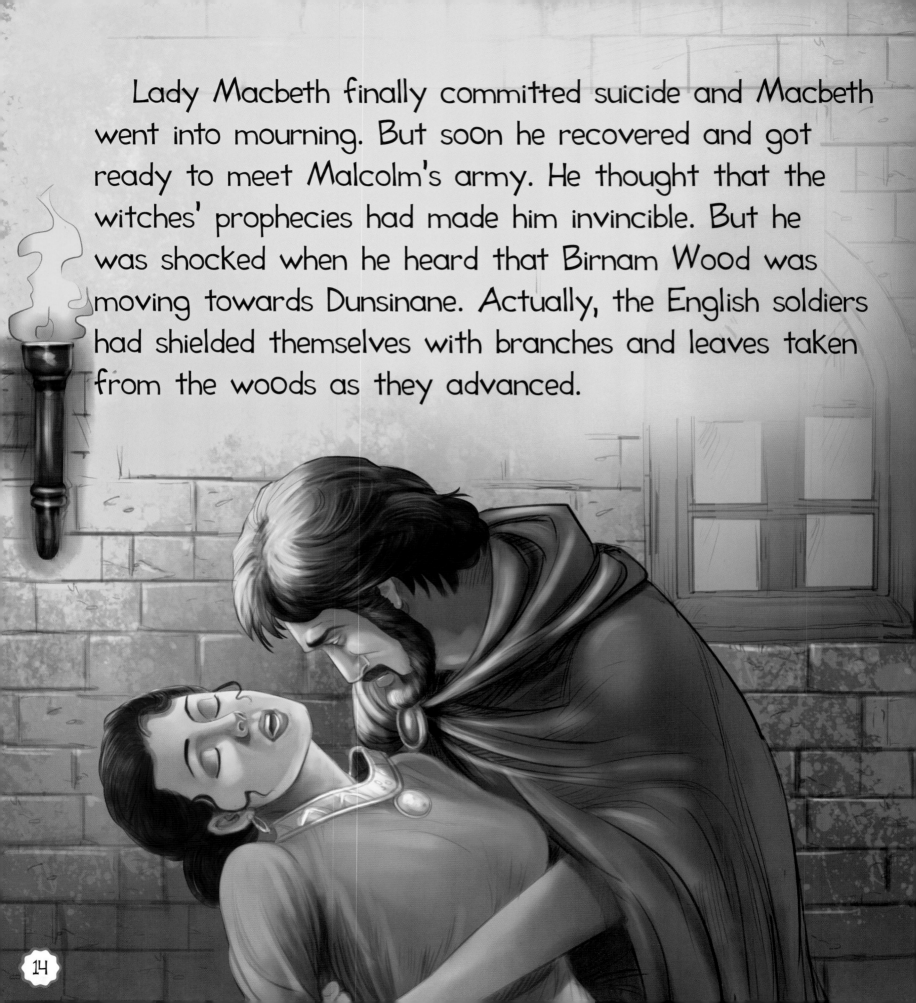

Macbeth fought bravely against Malcolm's army, but they defeated Macbeth's forces and captured his castle. As Macbeth met Macduff in battle, he realised that the witches had tricked him. Macduff told him about how he was ripped before time from his mother's body, and was not 'born of a woman' in the truest sense of the words.

"I am doomed!" Macbeth realised as he fought valiantly till he was killed by Macduff.

After Macbeth's death, Prince Malcolm was crowned King of Scotland at Scone amidst great celebrations throughout Scotland.

# The Merchant of Venice

An imprint of Om Books International

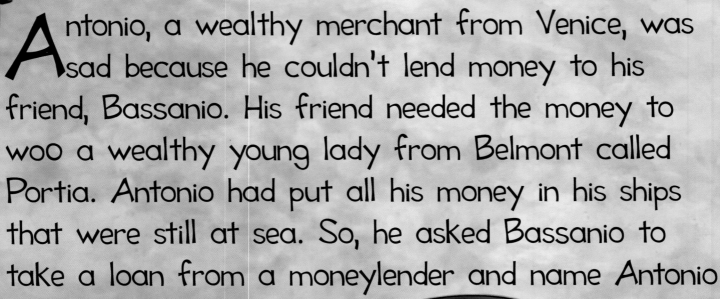

Antonio, a wealthy merchant from Venice, was sad because he couldn't lend money to his friend, Bassanio. His friend needed the money to woo a wealthy young lady from Belmont called Portia. Antonio had put all his money in his ships that were still at sea. So, he asked Bassanio to take a loan from a moneylender and name Antonio as guarantor.

But according to her father's will, Portia could only marry the man who chose the right casket out of the three her father had left behind. Portia didn't like any of her suitors and confessed to her lady-in-waiting, Nerissa, that she was in love with Bassanio.

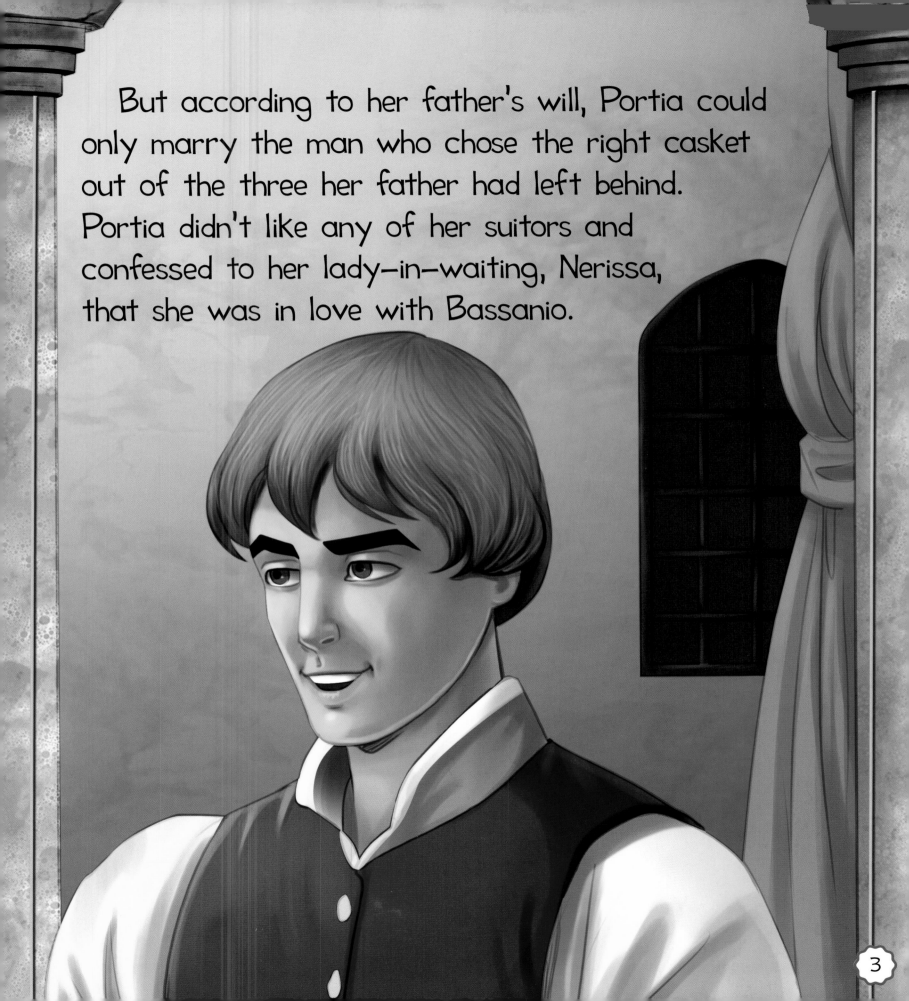

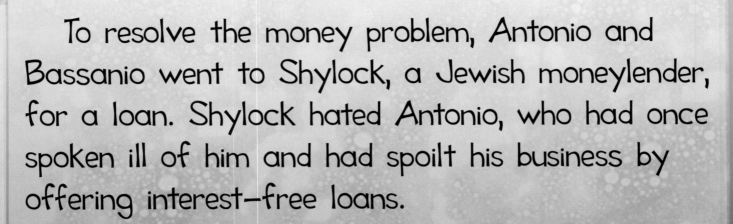

To resolve the money problem, Antonio and Bassanio went to Shylock, a Jewish moneylender, for a loan. Shylock hated Antonio, who had once spoken ill of him and had spoilt his business by offering interest-free loans.

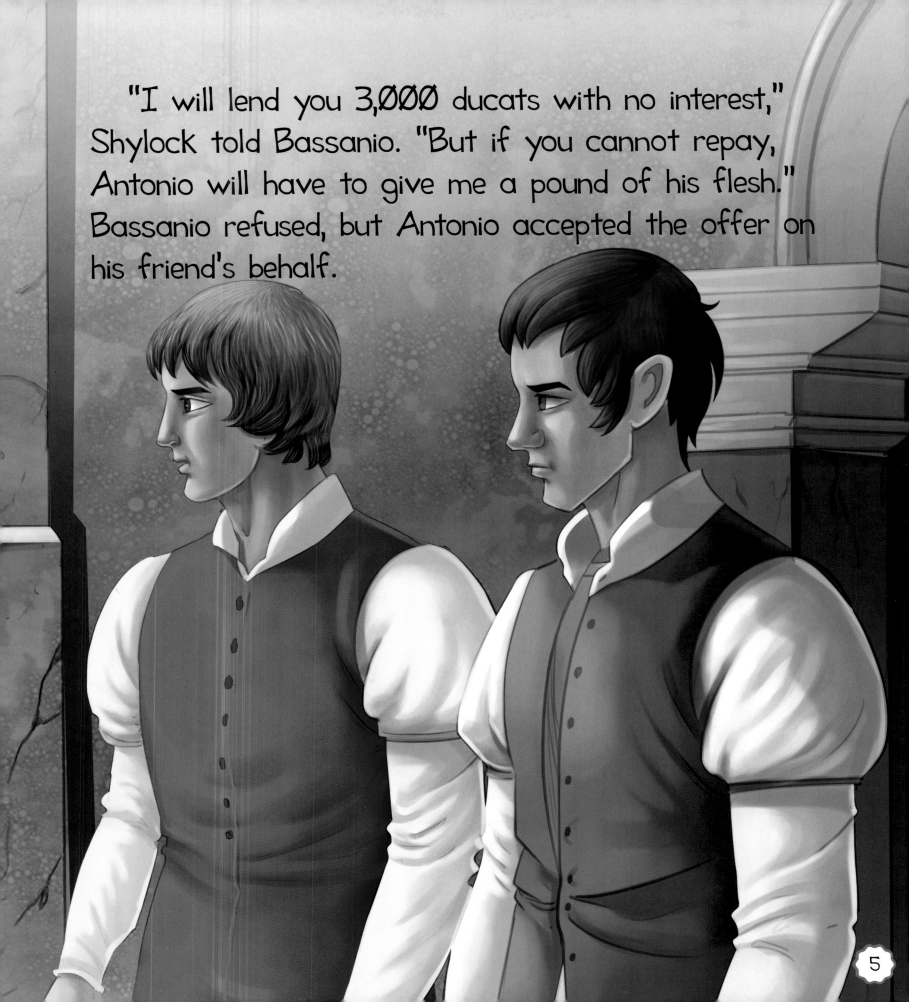

"I will lend you 3,000 ducats with no interest," Shylock told Bassanio. "But if you cannot repay, Antonio will have to give me a pound of his flesh." Bassanio refused, but Antonio accepted the offer on his friend's behalf.

Returning home, Shylock found out that his daughter Jessica had eloped with Bassanio's friend Lorenzo, but he also received some happy news that made his day. Shylock heard that Antonio's ships were lost at sea.

In Belmont, many suitors arrived to seek Portia's hand. One picked the golden casket and the other chose the silver casket, but they were all wrong.

Meanwhile, Bassanio reached Portia's estate with his friend, Gratiano. Bassanio and Portia confessed their love for each other. Bassanio chose the lead casket, which was the correct one. Gratiano proposed to Nerissa, who accepted him, and a double wedding was planned. Lorenzo and Jessica also joined them.

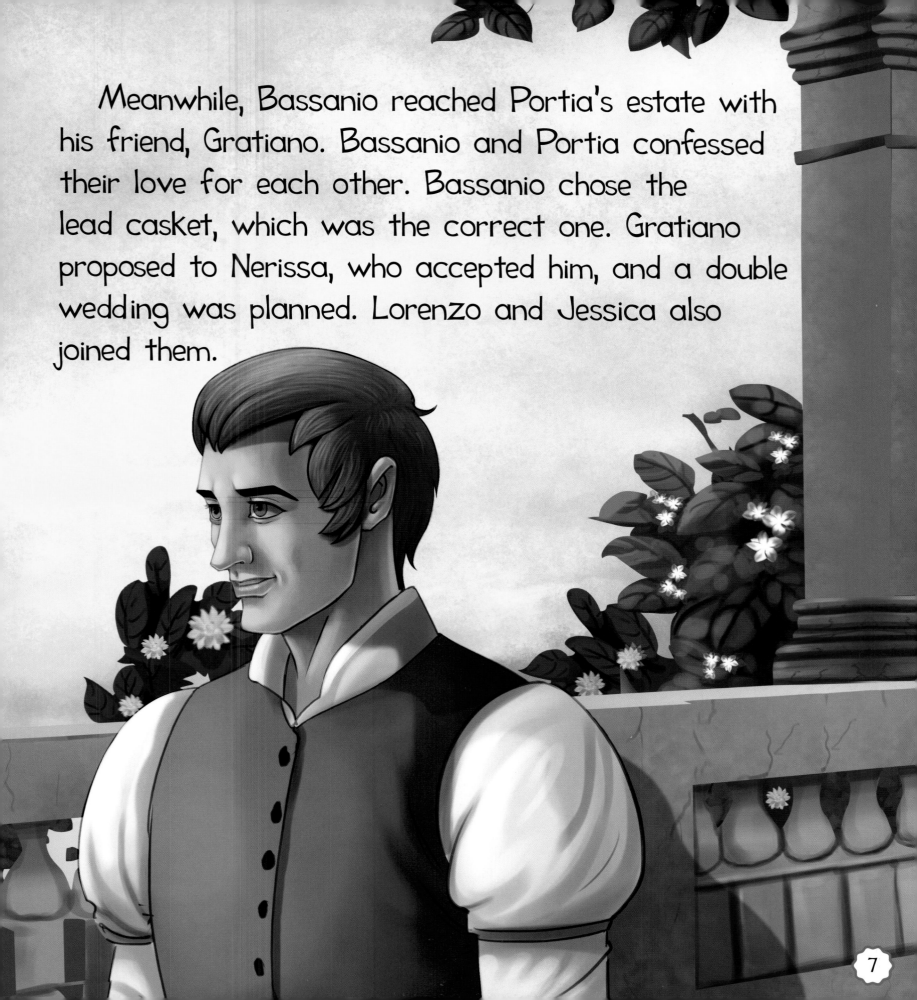

"Here is a token of my love!" Portia declared, handing Bassanio a golden ring. "You must never part with it."

As the couples celebrated, news arrived that Antonio had lost the ships and Shylock wanted to claim the debt. Bassanio and Gratiano immediately left for Venice. Worried, Portia and Nerissa decided to follow them disguised as men.

In Venice, Shylock refused to spare Antonio's life and the Duke of Venice called for a trial. He sent for a legal expert who was none other than Portia in disguise.

"The pound of flesh is rightfully mine," Shylock insisted even after Bassanio offered him twice the amount.

Portia examined the contract and said, "He is right."

Happy to have won, Shylock got ready to cut a pound of Antonio's flesh.

But Portia warned, "The pound of flesh is yours, but not his blood. You must cut the flesh without spilling any of the merchant's blood."

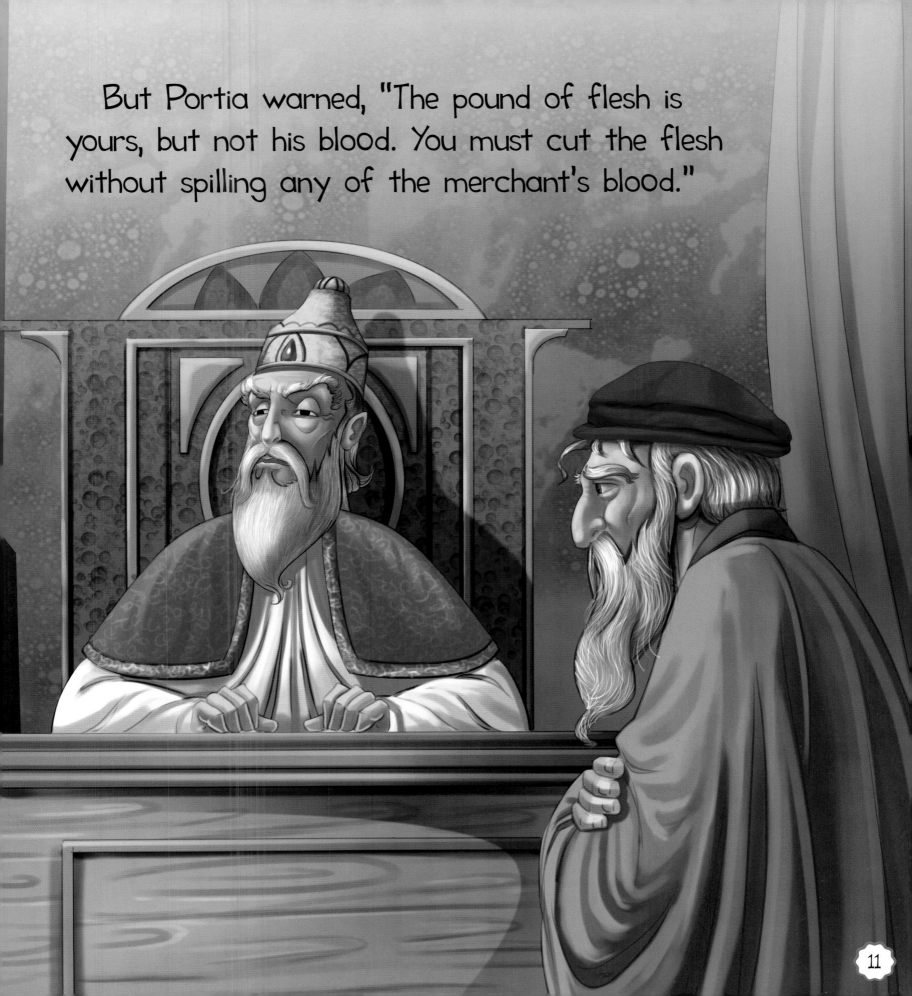

Shylock realised he had been trapped and said he would take the money instead.

"You must take what is in the contract or nothing," Portia declared. Shylock was silent, and she added, "You have tried to murder an honest man. Half your property will be confiscated, half shall go to Antonio."

The duke spared Shylock's life and Antonio agreed not to take away his property on two conditions: Shylock must become a Christian and leave all his wealth to Jessica and Lorenzo on his death. Shylock agreed.

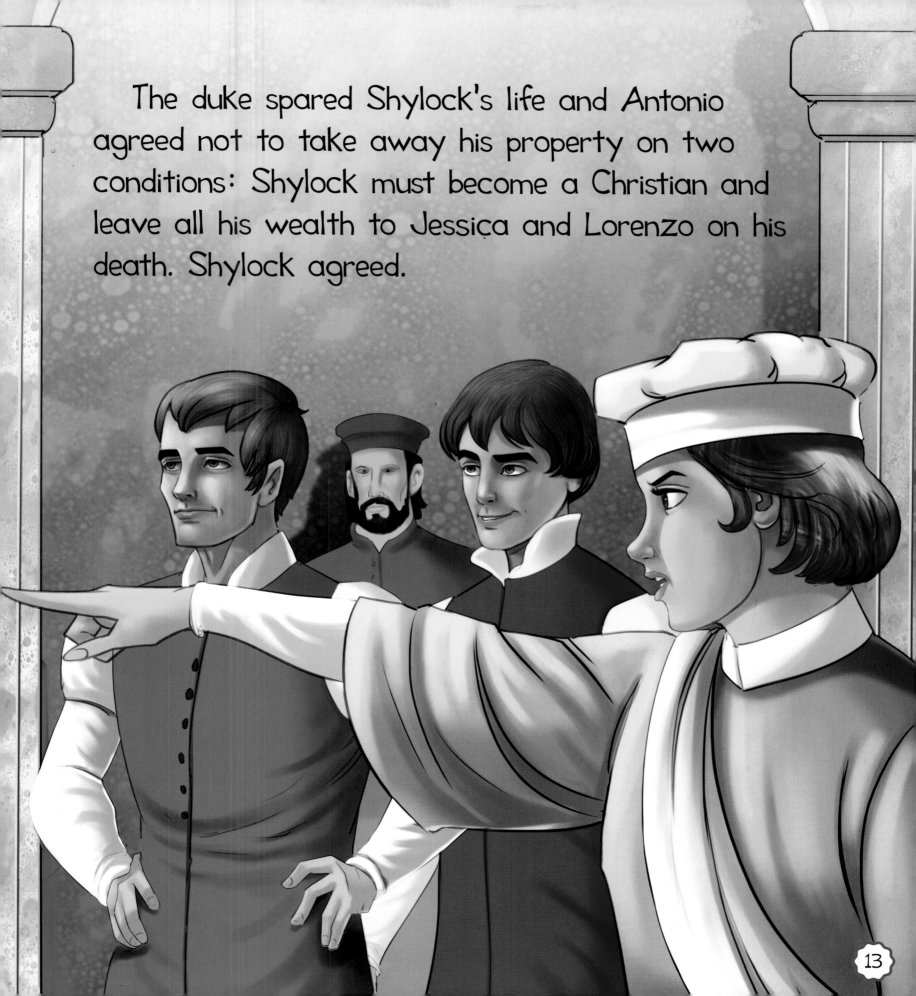

No one had recognised Portia.

Bassanio thanked Portia, the legal expert, and said, "Please accept a token of my gratitude."

Portia and Nerissa, who was disguised as a clerk, asked for the rings they had given to Bassanio and Gratiano. Both men did not recognise them and reluctantly gave them the rings. When the men reached Belmont, Portia and Nerissa pretended to be angry with them for losing the rings.

After some more play-acting, Portia revealed the truth. Bassanio was happy to know she had saved his friend. Jessica and Lorenzo were glad to hear of their inheritance. And Antonio's ships too arrived safely. Together, they celebrated their good fortune.

# Othello

An imprint of Om Books International

One night, on a Venetian street, Roderigo and Iago got into an argument. Roderigo had paid Iago to help him win Desdemona's hand, but she had married Othello, the Moorish general. Iago hated Othello because he had chosen Michael Cassio as lieutenant instead of him.

Meanwhile, Cassio arrived at Othello's house with a message.

The Duke needed Othello's help to defeat the Turks, who had invaded Cyprus. Just then, Brabanzio, Desdemona's father, arrived and accused Othello of kidnapping his daughter. On learning that Othello was going to meet the Duke, Brabanzio accompanied him so that he could complain about Othello. But there, Desdemona, the Duke and the senate supported Othello.

The Duke ordered Desdemona to accompany Othello to Cyprus. But on reaching Cyprus, they were informed that the Turkish navy had been destroyed in a storm at sea. There, Iago noticed Cassio holding Desdemona's hand in greeting and thought, "I must use this to my advantage."

"We shall celebrate tonight," Othello told Lodovico.

"I have no chance now," Roderigo said sadly to Iago before the night's festivities.

"Desdemona will soon lose interest in Othello," Iago assured him. "But first, you must ruin Cassio's reputation."

That night, Iago got Cassio drunk and Roderigo provoked Cassio into a fight. When Montano tried to stop Cassio, he injured Montano. Angry, Othello removed Cassio from his rank.

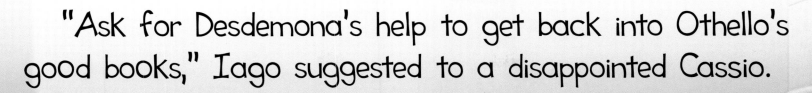

"Ask for Desdemona's help to get back into Othello's good books," Iago suggested to a disappointed Cassio.

Iago arranged for Cassio to meet Desdemona alone and she promised to help Cassio, but Othello and Iago arrived just when Cassio was talking to her. Cassio left without a word to Othello, leaving the latter jealous and suspicious.

Sensing an opportunity, Iago lied to Othello. He claimed that Cassio and Desdemona were in love. Later, when Desdemona pleaded with Othello, on behalf of Cassio, he got even more suspicious.

From that day on, Othello's behaviour towards Desdemona changed.

A few days later, when Desdemona discovered that Othello was unwell, she offered him her handkerchief. Iago's wife Emilia, pushed by Iago, stole the handkerchief.

Iago planted the handkerchief in Cassio's room and informed Othello that Cassio had Desdemona's handkerchief. Then, Othello asked Desdemona for the handkerchief, but she, of course, didn't have it.

Cassio wondered about the strange handkerchief and gave it to his friend, Bianca. Iago asked Othello to hide and overhear the conversation between him and Cassio. Iago asked questions about Bianca, without mentioning her name, but to Othello it appeared as if they were talking about Desdemona.

Later, the same day, Lodovico came from Venice with the Duke's letter, ordering Othello to return home and appointed Cassio as his replacement. In anger, Othello hit Desdemona and left the room.

Distraught over his behaviour, Desdemona asked Othello why he was angry and he accused Desdemona of being unfaithful. Meanwhile, Iago urged Roderigo to kill Cassio. But Roderigo was wounded by Cassio, and Iago injured Cassio in the dark and ran away. Later, in everyone's presence, Iago killed Roderigo for attacking Cassio.

Othello's rage now knew no bounds, and despite her pleas of innocence, he killed Desdemona. Just then, Emilia entered with the the news that Roderigo was dead, but Cassio was still alive.

"Desdemona was unfaithful! I have killed her," Othello confessed to Emilia. He added that Iago had told him about Desdemona's unfaithfulness.

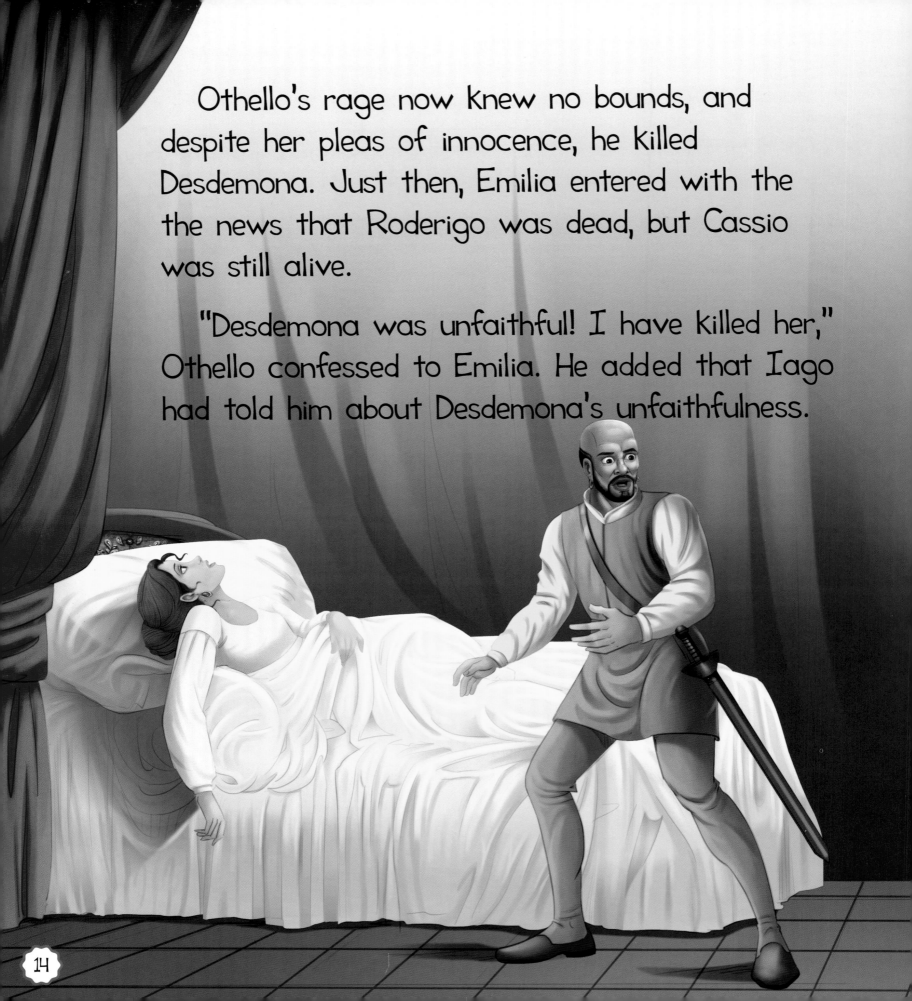

Just then, Montano and Iago too entered the room. Emilia told them that Desdemona had been innocent and she had been the one to give the handkerchief to Iago. An angry Othello tried to kill Iago, but instead, Iago killed Emilia and escaped.

However, he was soon captured and ordered to be executed.

15

"You must return to Venice and face trial," Lodovico informed Othello. But, grief-stricken and guilty, Othello chose to kill himself.

# Romeo and Juliet

An imprint of Om Books International

Once again, the servants of the warring Capulet and Montague families were brawling on the streets of Verona. Fed up, Prince Escalus, Verona's ruler, ordered that any person disturbing the city's peace be hanged.

2

Meanwhile, Montague's son, Romeo, confessed to his cousin Benvolio that he was in love with Rosaline, who did not return his love.

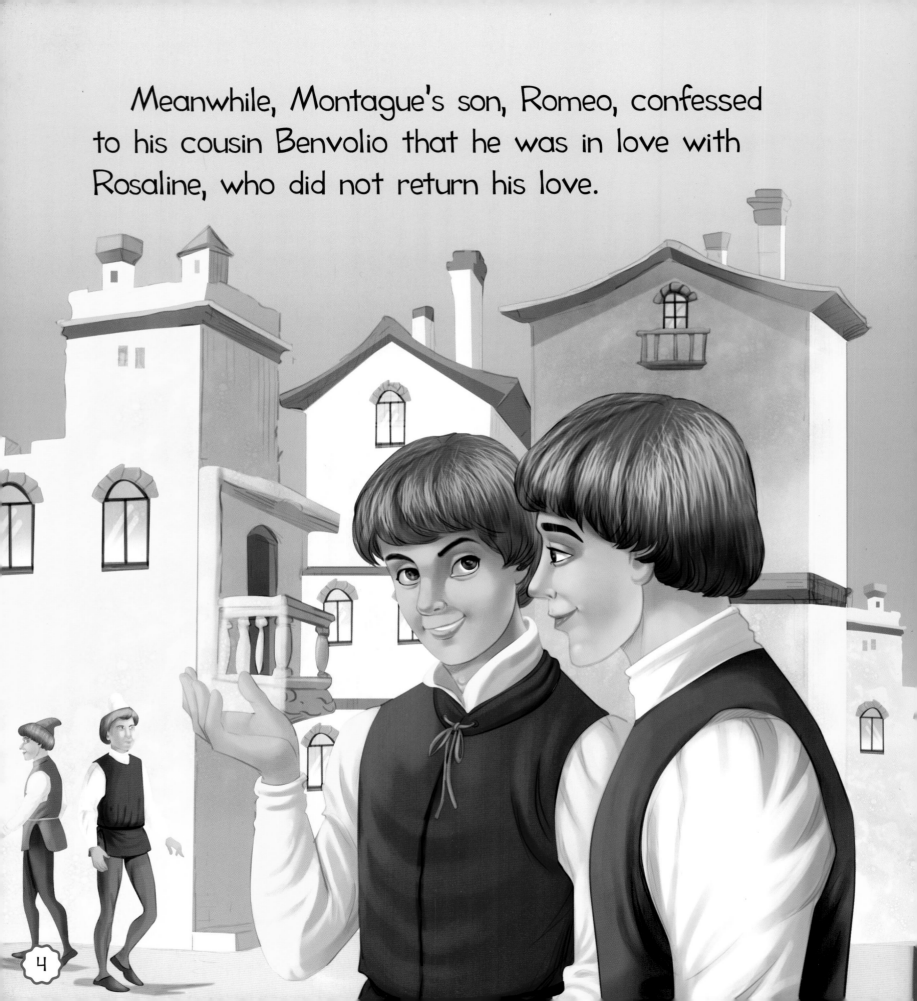

One of the king's kinsmen, Paris, asked Capulet for his daughter, Juliet's hand in marriage. Capulet decided to invite Paris for a masquerade, hoping that Juliet would fall in love with Paris.

Meanwhile, Romeo and Benvolio bumped into a Capulet servant carrying the invitation list. Benvolio urged Romeo to sneak into the masquerade ball.

Romeo, Benvolio and their friend Mercutio attended the masquerade ball. Romeo saw Juliet there and fell in love with her at first sight, forgetting all about Rosaline.

However, a Capulet, Tybalt, recognised Romeo.

"How dare a Montague enter our house?" Tybalt asked angrily, but another Capulet stopped him from creating a ruckus at the feast.

Romeo and Juliet were instantly attracted to each other and fell in love. But soon, they realised that their fathers were sworn enemies. Later, Romeo leaped the wall and landed in Juliet's garden. He saw Juliet on her balcony.

"Juliet!" Romeo cried, and the two promised to love each other forever.

Soon, Romeo met his friend, Friar Lawrence, who agreed to marry the lovers in secret. And the next day, Romeo and Juliet were married.

Though Tybalt didn't know anything about their marriage, he challenged Romeo to a duel. But Romeo did not want to fight him. Instead, Mercutio fought with Tybalt. Mercutio was killed and an angry Romeo murdered Tybalt. Enraged, the Prince banished Romeo to Mantua.

Few days later, Juliet learnt that her father wanted her to marry Paris. She rushed to Friar Lawrence, who planned to reunite the pair in Mantua.

"You must drink this potion that will make you appear dead," he told Juliet. "We'll come and get you, once you are buried. Then, you will be united with Romeo forever."

Juliet returned home to discover that her wedding to Paris had been fixed for the next day. Juliet drank the potion and the next morning everyone thought she was dead. The Capulets buried Juliet in the family tomb. But Friar Lawrence's messenger never reached Mantua and Romeo only received the news of Juliet's death.

"I would rather die than live without Juliet," Romeo decided and bought a vial of poison.

He rushed to Juliet's tomb, on which Paris was scattering flowers. An angry Romeo killed Paris. He entered the tomb and saw Juliet's body. Grief-stricken to see his beloved's body, Romeo drank the poison and died by her side.

Just then, Friar Lawrence entered the tomb and was shocked to see Romeo dead. Juliet too rose and was stunned. She refused to leave when the Friar fled. Devastated, Juliet killed herself with Romeo's dagger.

Soon, the Prince, the Capulets and the
Montagues arrived and saw the lovers lying dead.
The two families finally agreed to end the feud
and built statues of their children in Verona.